RICE
PIE
and
MOSES

JOHN RICE,
PIE CORBETT
and
BRIAN MOSES

ILLUSTRATED BY
WOODY

Macmillan Children's Books

First published 1995 by
Macmillan Children's Books
a division of Macmillan Publishers Ltd
Cavaye Place London SW10 9PG
and Basingstoke

Associated companies throughout the world

ISBN 0 330 33874 9

9 8 7 6 5 4 3 2 1

A CIP catalogue record for this book is available from the British Library.

Typeset in 11/14 Monophoto Gill Sans
Printed by Cox & Wyman Ltd, Reading

Grateful permission is acknowledged for the use of Wings on p57
previously published by OUP in Another First Poetry Book.

CONTENTS

Rice

Pie

Moses

Rice

If . . .

If ships sailed on the motorway
    and potato crisps were blue,
if football boots were made of silk
    and a lamppost wore a shoe.

If motorbikes ran upwards
    and milk floats really floated,
if beds were full of dinosaurs
    and peas were sugar-coated.

If flies wore bomber-jackets
    and eggs laid little chickens,
if spacemen had a panther each
    and insects studied Dickens.

If babies' prams were motorized
    and you listened to your conscience,
if your brain was working properly
    you wouldn't read this nonscience.

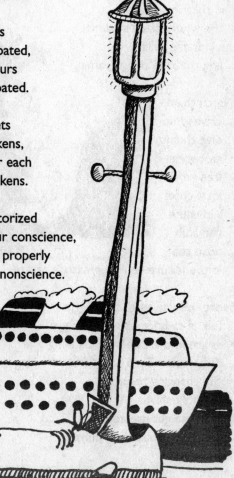

Leisure Centre, Pleasure Centre

You go through plate glass doors
   with giant red handles,
into light that's as bright
   as a million candles.
The chlorine smells
   the whole place steaming,
the kids are yelling
   and the kids are screaming.

Watch them
   wave jump
   dive thump
   cartwheel
   free wheel
   look cute
   slip chute
   toe stub
   nose rub

in the leisure centre, pleasure centre.

Sporty people laugh and giggle
   folk in swim suits give a wiggle.
Kids are in the cafe busy thinking
   if they can afford some fizzy drinking.
In the changing rooms
   wet folk shiver
It's hard to get dressed
   when you shake and quiver.

And we go
  breast stroke
  back stroke
  two stroke
  big folk
  hair soak
  little folk
  eye poke
  no joke
  in the leisure centre, pleasure centre.

And now we're driving back home
  fish'n'chips in the car,
eyes are slowly closing
  but it's not very far.
Snuggle wuggle up in fresh clean sheets
  a leisure centre trip
is the best of treats

because you can
  keep fit
  leap sit
  eat crisps
  do twists
  belly flop
  pit stop
  fill up
  with 7-Up
  get going
  blood flowing
  look snappy
  be happy
  in the leisure centre, pleasure centre.

Big Fears

Twenty-five feet above Sian's house
hangs a thick wire cable
that droops and sags between
two electricity pylons.

A notice says it carries 320,000 volts
from one metallic scarecrow to the next,
then on to the next and the next
right across the countryside to the city.
The cable sways above Sian's council house
making her radio crackle and sometimes
making her television go on the blink.

If it's a very windy night
Sian gets frightened because
she thinks the cable might snap,
fall on to the roof and electrocute
everyone as they sleep.

This is Sian's Big Fear.

Outside Matthew's bedroom there
is a tall tree – taller than the house.
In summer it is heavy with huge leaves.
In winter it stands lonely as a morning moon.

On a windy night Matthew worries
that the tree might be blown down
and crash through his bedroom window.
It would certainly kill him and his cat
if it was sleeping under the bed
where it usually goes.

This is Matthew's Big Fear.

Outside Karen's bedroom there's nothing
but a pleasant view: meadows, hedges, sheep
and some distant gentle hills.
There's nothing sinister, nothing to worry about.

But at night, in the dark, Karen thinks
the darting shapes on the ceiling
are really the shadows of a ghost's
great cold hands and that the night noises
made by the water pipes are
the screeches and groans of attic skeletons.

Bats at Evening

Under the husk
   of a Scottish dusk
black bats scatter.

At high pine height
   splitting the night
they dart and clatter.

They shake the lake
   bank and brake
as the shadows shatter.

And as damp dark falls
   they cancel their calls
– a midge meal fatter!

The Mysteries of Nature
or Globular Bunkular My Duck Has Sunkular

Nature poems are popular
but seldom very jocular.
But this one is spectacular
because it's quite funicular.

Let's take a country walkular
through fields that are rusticular.
Look through your binocular,
– there's an eagle and a hawkular!

The hedgerow in particular
is a home so very insular
for creatures shaped triangular
or even semicircular.

You may come across a spookular
in the forest deep and darkular.
A sharp stab in your jugular
means you've met up with Count Dracula!

By the church that looks so secular
is a pond where you'll find duckular.
This one doesn't quackular
since it argued with a truckular!

I see by the town clockular
that time is passing quickular.
I think we need a breakular,
– too much nature makes you sickular!

Ghost Hunt

Long after midnight (whoo-whoo)
I searched for the haunted house (whoo-whoo),
but I didn't see
    a speck of a spectre
    a fraction of a phantom
    a spot of a spook
    a pinch of a poltergeist.
I didn't even catch the sweet scent
of a skellington's wellingtons!

Long after midnight (whoo-whoo)
I searched for the haunted house (whoo-whoo)
but when I couldn't find it
– well, I just gave up the ghost.

White Kite

White kite
at night
in flight
at height
star light
moon bright
white kite
some sight
held tight
with
all
my
m
i
g
h
t
.
.
.
.
.
.
.
.
.

Instructions for Giants

Please do not step on swing parks, youth clubs
   cinemas or discos.
Please flatten all schools!

Please do not eat children, pop stars, TV soap actors,
   kind grannies who give us 50p.
Please feel free to gobble up dentists and teachers
   any time you like!

Please do not block out the sunshine.
Please push all rain clouds over to France.

Please do not drink the public swimming pool.
Please eat all cabbage fields, vegetable plots
   and anything green that grows in the
     boring countryside!

Please do not trample kittens, lambs or other baby animals.
Please take spiders and snakes, ants and beetles home for
   your own pets.

Please stand clear of jets passing.
Please sew up the ozone layer.
Please mind where you're putting your big feet –
and no sneaking off to China when we're playing
   hide-and-seek!

Gorbelly Goes Shopping

When Gorbelly the Giant goes shopping
at the Superhypermegamarket,
he carries a monstrous, megalithic, monumental
plastic bag, and he buys

ten thousand Titanic-sized tins
of processed people

countless colossal cans of baked beings

a billion bulky bottles of humanade

piles of paunchy packets of folk fingers

hugely ginormous jars of pickled persons

a hundred Herculean cartons of children chunks

twenty-a-plenty podgy portions of pensioner pieces

six thousand strapping slices of grilled grown-ups.

Gorbelly's shopping list is as long as
an airport runway. He uses a jumbo jet
as a shopping trolley.

On his way home he often picks up
a theme park or a fairground to give
to his little son Gorbellybutton as a present.

21

Mr Body, the Head

**(How many parts of the body can you spot in this poem?
If you find them all, give yourself a big hand!)**

Our Head, Mr Body, is six feet tall.
He's always on his toes and has a heart of gold.
He has a finger in every pie
and a chip on his shoulder.

He doesn't stand for any cheek
and so we don't give him any lip
and we don't talk back.

Mr Body knows when we're pulling his leg
and he says, "Hold your tongue.
Just you knuckle down and toe the line.
I want no underhand tricks in my school."

He says our new school
cost an arm and a leg to build.
He had to fight for it tooth and nail.

Mr Body says he shoulders the burden
of responsibility and he ends up
doing the work of four people.

That must make him . . . a forehead!

A Man Was in His Room

A man was in his room:
all of a suddlington
he jumped off his bed
almost knocking over
the lamp that stood on the small table.

He heaved off his boots and socks
throwing them wildly behind him.
Then he rolled up the legs
of his white jeans,
went out and paddled in the pink sunset.

Everyone watched in amazement.

Photographers click-clicked as he ran
from purple cloud to orange cloud
and a vicar clasped his hands in prayer.

When he got back,
he walked through the crowds of people
who had been watching him.

Television reporters tried to get him
to say a few words into their microphones
but he only smiled and pointed to his toes
which were singing and dancing
all by themselves.

Dinosaur Day

What sight do you see when you look at his neck?
      Did Dinah sword-dance on dinosaur day?

A rubbery tube of brown and black speck.
      Yes, Dinah sword-danced on dinosaur day.

What view do you get when you look at his head?
      Did Dinah sword-dance on dinosaur day?

A sharp cutting gap and two deep wells of red.
      Yes, Dinah sword-danced on dinosaur day.

What can your eyes tell when you look at his tail?
      Did Dinah sword-dance on dinosaur day?

An engine of force to help him set sail.
      Yes, Dinah sword-danced on dinosaur day.

What shape can you spy when you stare at his leg?
      Did Dinah sword-dance on dinosaur day?

A 'Z' and an 'S' both as smooth as an egg.
      Yes, Dinah sword-danced on dinosaur day.

Spy neck, spy speck, see head, see red.
      sight tail, sight sail, spot egg, spot leg.

The beasts of the sea sang the words of the bay
      When Dinah sword-danced on dinosaur day.

Brokendown Countdown

Tense

Nice

Ates

Sonce

Sykes

Fice

Force

Thrice

Twice

Wonce

Nunce!

Dazzledance
(for Heather)

I have an eye of silver,
I have an eye of gold,
I have a tongue of reed-grass
   and a story to be told.

I have a hand of metal,
I have a hand of clay,
I have two arms of granite
   and a song for every day.

I have a foot of damson,
I have a foot of corn,
I have two legs of leaf-stalk
   and a dance as yet unborn.

I have a dream of water,
I have a dream of snow,
I have a thought of wildfire
   and a harp-string long and low.

I have an eye of silver,
I have an eye of gold,
I have a tongue of reed-grass
   and a story to be told.

The Man, the Moon and the Microlight

High up high
on his way to who cares where,
a goggled man aboard an insect.
Pepper-white wings against a darkening sky
high up high.

High up high
on his way to who says where
a marching moon in a middle time.
Silver paper circle against the darkening sky
high up high.

Diamond Rattlesnake

Her tough skin glistens
in the burning sunlight.
Dark raisin eyes sparkle –
fangs like curved icicles.

She traces an 'S' across the sand
leaving picture patterns.
A writing, slithering lasso
on her slow journey to wherever.

Arching like a gymnast,
curving like a living rainbow,
no instrument can match her music.

I Planted a Tree, I Planted a Poem

I planted a tree.
Its branches swept the bright sky,
its roots gripped the dark earth.
Birds hid deep within its foliage,
its leaves blossomed and fell.

I planted a poem.
Its song swept the bright sky,
its words gripped the dark earth.
Ideas hid within its lines,
its truth blossomed and fell.

My Favourite Thingummybob

My favourite colour is 'W',
my favourite drink is bees.
My favourite song is an apple,
my favourite place is trees.

My favourite flower is bottle,
my favourite book is socks.
My favourite sweets are forty,
my favourite game is a fox.

My favourite pet is a teaspoon,
my favourite friend is a clock.
My favourite clothes are biscuits
any my favourite word is
       S P L O C K!!!

Ettykett

My mother knew a lot about manners,
    she said you should never slurp;
you should hold your saucer firmly,
    and not clang your teeth on the curp.

My father knew nothing of manners,
    all he could do was slurp;
and when I can't find a rhyming word,
    I set about making them urp.

Bears Don't Like Bananas

Monkeys like to play the drums,
    badgers wear bandanas.
Tigers like to tickle toes
    but bears don't like bananas.

A crocodile can juggle buns
    on visits to his nana's.
Seagulls like to dance and sing
    but bears don't like bananas.

Rats and mice can somersault
    and do gymnastics with iguanas.
Weasels like to wiggle legs
    but bears don't like bananas.

A porcupine likes drinking tea,
    and cheering at gymkhanas.
A ladybird likes eating pies
    but bears don't like bananas.

Pie

Poetman

The Poetman
calls at each house
in the early hours.

When the stars are frosted flowers
and the night a velvet mole.

The Poetman shoulders his bundle –

At each doorstep
he sheds a poem or two.

His whistle surprises the dark.
Like a waking spell.

Dogs bark back a greeting.
Cats arch and purr.

In bedrooms children stir.
The moon grins

a thin-lipped smile.
Sleepy poems like fragile reptiles

slither indoors.
Still curled in our beds

our dreamy heads catch
the sound of their snores.

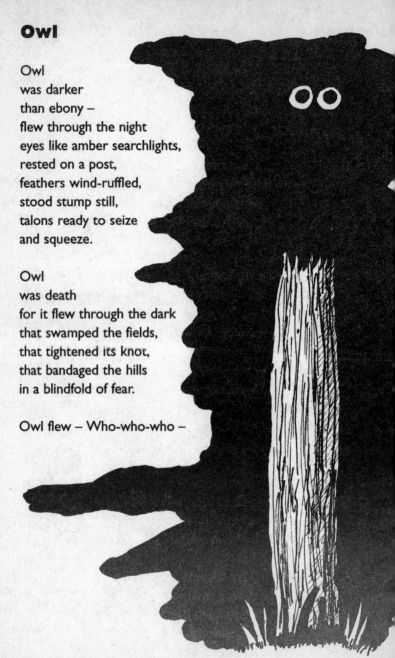

Owl

Owl
was darker
than ebony –
flew through the night
eyes like amber searchlights,
rested on a post,
feathers wind-ruffled,
stood stump still,
talons ready to seize
and squeeze.

Owl
was death
for it flew through the dark
that swamped the fields,
that tightened its knot,
that bandaged the hills
in a blindfold of fear.

Owl flew – Who-who-who –

Outbreak of Peace Haiku

My mum declares peace.
She hands out bouquets of smiles.
Laughter like church bells.

An Odd Kettle of Fish

1   The detectives said that
The books had been cooked.
(They tasted good.)

2   My teacher said we could
have a free hand.
(I added it to my collection.)

3   Some people bottle up
their feelings.
(I keep mine in a jar.)

4   My mother said –
'Hold your tongue!'
(It was too slippery.)

5   When my sister laughs
she drives me round the bend.
(I catch the bus back.)

6   Dad told me
to keep a stiff upper lip.
(It's in a box by my bed.)

7   My Uncle is a terrible
name-dropper.
(I help my Aunt to sweep them up.)

8   In the school races
I licked everyone in the class.
(It made my tongue sore.)

Scarecrow Christmas

In winter fields
a scarecrow sings
the hopeful tune
of lonely kings.

His empty heart
is thin and cold.
his cruel rags
are worn and old.

But in our homes
we sing out clear,
warm words of joy
and know no fear.

In bed at night
we listen for
padded footsteps
at the door.

In other fields
and different lands,
living scarecrows
reach out hands.

They live beneath
the sun's cruel rays.
They do not know
of Christmas days.

Grotty Borlotti

Mum went to a lecture and gave up meat.
Now she dishes up beans, 'just for a treat',
we get –

Creamy bran chunks or buckwheat bake,
brandied prune mousse and carrot cake.

Hazelnut tart with stir-fried cheese,
garlic salad and herbal teas.

Mushroom pate and split pea spread,
soya burger on curried bread.

Wholemeal pasta and a broad bean nutlet,
cashew nut soup and a chick pea cutlet.

Continental lentils or rice on toast,
grotty borlotti and dreaded nut roast.

Coconut chutney and beanshoot fritters,
It's boring beans that give us the jitters.

So, Dad and I took up jogging,
just down to the end of the street.
For it isn't too far
to the Hamburger Bar,
where, 'just for a treat',
we'll stop –
and eat meat.

A Chance in France

'Stay at home,'
Mum said.

But I –
took a chance
in France,
turned grey
for the day
in St Tropez,
I forgot
what I did
in Madrid,
had some tussles
in Brussels
with a trio
from Rio,
lost my way
in Bombay,
nothing wrong
in Hong Kong,
felt calmer
in Palma,
and quite nice
in Nice,
yes, felt finer
in China,
took a room
in Khartoum
and a villa

in Manilla,
had a 'do'
in Peru
with a Llama
from Lima,
took a walk
in New York
with a man
from Milan,
lost a sneaker
in Costa Rica,
got lumbago
in Tobago,
felt a menace
in Venice,
was a bore
in Singapore,
lost an ear
in Korea
some weight
in Kuwait,
tried my best
as a guest
in old Bucharest,
got the fleas
in Belize
and came home.

Ear Poem

They sit on the side
of your face —
would look out of place
stuck somewhere else —
on your bottom
would not look right.
I suppose a bottom ear
would be a rear ear.
They're good for
holding glasses up
and picking
when you're bored.
Some people keep
orange waxy bits
stored inside them.
Mothers peer
into ears,
searching for
tell-tale signs of dirt —
or they poke about
behind them
to find where
you haven't washed
for weeks.
And teachers
have been known
to tug the squashed ears
of small boys
who are rude
or have been caught
flicking food
at meal times.

Noddy's friend,
Big Ears, had whoppers –
so too do coppers.
They need to keep
their ears close to the ground.
Elephants have ears
like canvas sails.
But whales don't seem
to have ears at all.
What I fear most about my ears
is that someone will
chop them off and leave me earless.
But if I could unscrew my ears
and buy new ones I'd be fearless.
I'd swagger into the local Ear Shop
and order, 'a bag
of assorted ears, please' –
an ear for every occasion.
Then if I got a flea in my ear
I could just swap it over.

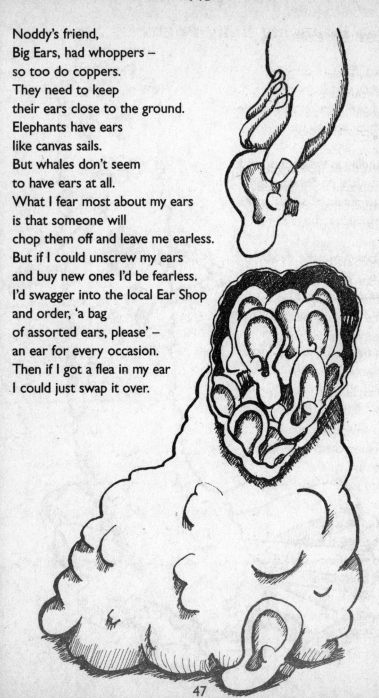

The Bouncing Belly Poem

I ran into the chippie
to buy us fish 'n' chips
and saw a battered sausage
putting lipstick on its lips.

Standing in the Laundromat
quite late on Sunday night
I saw a pair of purple pants
go spinning out of sight.

I nipped into the pet shop
to buy a furry chum.
I chose a big gorilla
that looked just like my mum.

I dashed around the corner
to buy a little jelly.
I slipped on a banana skin
and bounced upon my belly.

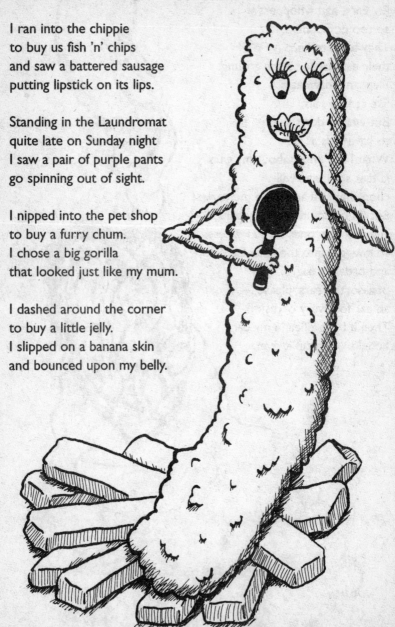

A Scrambled Poem

Sheep are sheepish,
rams can ramble.
Hares are hairy
but eggs get scrambled.

Cats have catastrophes,
dogs are dogged
Cheetahs can cheat
but fleas are horrid.

Slugs are sluggish
and bees get beaten,
cows are cowards
but pigs get eaten.

The Playground Monster

It grabbed me
with its tarmac jaws
and then it tried
to bite me.

It grasped me
with its gravelly paws
and then it tried
to fight me.

I live in fear of walking
across its great black back.

I think it knows I'm talking.
It listens at a crack!

I fear its greedy darkness,
the way it seems to need

to reach out when I'm running
and grab me for a feed.

It grabbed me
with its tarmac jaws
and then it tried
to bite me.

It grasped me
with its gravelly paws
and then it tried
to fight me.

Heaven's Market

Sure, I dreamt of Heaven —
that market in the sky —
queues of smiling shoppers
all hoping they could buy

A brand new heart for grandad,
his old one can't keep time,
a zoo without the bars
where a cage would be a crime.

Some sharp eyes for my auntie,
her old ones both wore thin,
new shoes that never tire
and some races you can win.

Fresh Ethiopian rain,
a dad for Cushla too,
books that read themselves
and a sky that's always blue.

A stranger's smile that means it,
a pet that cannot die,
balloons that never burst
bright words that never lie.

Conker Crazy

Once a year
the craze came round –
we'd chuck sticks
into the big conker tree
by Samways Lane
and scrabble for
king-sized prizes.
  'Iddy, iddy onker,
  my first conker.
  Iddy, iddy ack,
  my first whack,'
we'd chant.
Taking a crack
on the knuckles
was part of the game.
Each breaktime
we'd gather by the sheds
to try to make
our chosen conker
up to a 'tenner' –
Some talked of
stewed conkers
dipped in vinegar,
others buried them
till they turned black.
My friend Donald
told stories of a king conker,
an invincible ace,
that his dad had owned.
Too often I'd end up
with tangled strings
or halves in the gutter.

On the way back home
I'd mutter to my brothers
of a dream conker,
hard as concrete,
that I'd stash away
for a year or two.
Then I'd return,
conker crazy,
to St Peter's Primary
ready to take my revenge.

Holidays

We never went
anywhere exotic –
best friends' parents picked
faraway places,
came back with suntanned faces
from Malaga and Malibu,
knew how to avoid jet lag.
Their bags labelled
with names that breathed magic.
From Rotterdam to Panama
my friends flew – True,
my family enjoyed
our fortnight out in tents.
True, we were glad to cook
on an open fire,
often with dire consequences.
True, we never seemed to tire
of the ghost moon
and bright stars
like ancient runes
whose patterns we read.
We'd come home dirty,
begging for a decent bed –
While our friends, hotel pampered,
smelt of lotion,
and their talk made us wish for
distant oceans, sands and palm trees;
we'd taste the scented breeze
of our foreign dream.

Strange then, how friends
seemed to prefer two weeks,
stuck beneath canvas,
of rough wind, rain and sun.
Two weeks to feel.
To rediscover something real.

Smelling Rats

My mother said she'd 'smelt a rat',
but none of us knew what she meant.
I wondered what a rat smelt like –
They lived in sewers, Sarah said,
where they grew big as tom cats,
if cornered would go for the throat.
They made brief film appearances,
dancing on Dracula's coffin,
Gangsters muttered, 'you dirty rat',
scientists kept them in cages,
testing lipstick and disease.
They ran on to boats up anchor lines
and of course we all knew
that they carried the plague.
Bubonic plague.
'BEW BON NICK . . .'
We whispered the words
so Mum wouldn't hear,
and sniffed deep
but, smelt nothing.

So we left her to hunt for the rat
and ran down the garden calling,
'Bring out your dead!'
Later that night I lay in bed,
and heard the dread sound
of whatever it was that she sensed.
I lay in the dark
and sniffed . . .

Wings

If I had wings
  I would touch the fingertips of clouds
    and glide on the wind's breath.

If I had wings
  I would taste a chunk of the sun
    as hot as peppered curry.

If I had wings
  I would listen to the clouds of sheep bleat
    that graze on the blue.

If I had wings
  I would breathe deep and sniff
    the scent of raindrops.

If I had wings
  I would gaze at the people
    who cling to the earth's crust.

If I had wings
  I would dream of
    swimming the deserts
      and walking the seas.

Kicking Turf

I knew that I would never be
among those chosen first –
I'd sit while the captains picked
and waited for the worst –
stuck in the last three –
with Ollie, fat and slow,
Binns, tall and weak,
and myself,
'a physique somewhat lacking'
our headteacher said.

So, Ollie, Binns and I
played at the back.
We watched the others,
football lovers,
dash forwards to score
more cracking goals.
While Ollie, Binns and I
strolled about,
kicking chunks of earth
at each other –
till the other side
tore up the turf
towards us
with the ball skidding
to the goal
where Ollie waited
to dive and roll,
his gloved fists clenched.
From the bench
Mr Wheeler roared at us.

And if they scored,
which they often did,
our side, our team –
who liked to be up front,
well stuck in –
would roll their eyes skywards
or shout at us
for all they were worth.
While Ollie, Binns and I
went back to kicking turf.

The Kiss

We'd been flicking through
The Guinness Book of records -
when Joanna found that
the world's longest kiss
had been for seventeen days,
in Chicago, USA.
That's what started the craze
for long distance kissing.
I kept well away
till one day I was cornered
by the school's professional
out for a spot of practice —
She said —
come on give us a kiss.
I said —
YUCK, no way, José.
She said —
come on give us a kiss.
I said —
No way, Shirley whirley.
I'm off —
and I legged it
to the end of the playground
where she pursued me
whooping and yelling
like a siren
with lips like suction pads
and octopus arms that made a grab.

So I legged it
to the bicycle sheds
where she followed me
with lips like a frog
and said –
Come on give us a snog.
So I said –
No way, not today.
And I legged it
to the drinking fountain in the hall
where she tracked me down
with a frown
and lips puckered
ready to kiss me to death.
She said –
come on, let's break the record.
So I thought –
why not
and said OK then.
But it was she who scarpered
quick as a knife
to the other end of the playground
where she told
my best friend Petie Fisher
that I was her boyfriend
and wanted a kiss.

I've decided that kissing
is no good for your health.
I'm keeping my lips
for the nicest person I know.
Me.

My Brother's Pig

Who – Grew till he was longer than a door.
      With big yellow tusks like handles.

Was – Big and bulky as baggage for India.
      With skin as tough as canvas.

His – Hairs as rough as a stiff brush.
      And a corkscrew for a tail.

Friend – That grunted a muddy welcome.
      Crunched acorns like boiled sweets.

And – He lay like a Walrus alone
      in the hot dark of his shed.

Strange – That he whistled when he blew
      bubbles of spit from his nose.

Pet – Better than a goldfish.
      For at night he crunched chunks
      from the stars.

City Jungle

Rain splinters town.

Lizard cars cruise by;
their radiators grin.

Thin headlights stare —
shop doorways keep
their mouths shut.

At the roadside
hunched houses cough.

Newspapers shuffle by,
hands in their pockets.
The gutter gargles.

A motorbike snarls;
dustbins flinch.

Streetlights bare
their yellow teeth.
The motorway's cat-black tongue
lashes across
the glistening back
of the tarmac night.

Moses

The Wrong Side

My mother used to tell me
I'd got out of bed
on the wrong side, which was strange
as there was only one side
I could tumble from.

The other was hard against the wall
and all I did was bang
my knee, but still she insisted
that she was right.
So one bright morning
I tried it out, squeezed
between the wall and my bed,
then said nothing.
She never knew, I was puzzled.

My mother said how she'd teach me
to choose between wrong and right,
but if I got out the right side
and that was wrong,
then who was right?

Don't You Know There's a War On?

My mother didn't know there was a war on!
She hung out her washing on the line
as I crouched among the cabbages
and gave covering fire.

My father didn't know there was a war on!
He called out 'Hello' as he came back from work
and I broke cover, shouted back,
ignoring the cracking of bullets.

The dog didn't know there was a war on!
He carried on sniffing in No Man's Land
then cocked a leg on the sign I'd painted
to warn of the danger from mines.

The neighbours didn't know there was a war on!
They hung over our fence and complained
that one of my missiles went AWOL
and drove its way through the dahlias.

After that I jacked in the war,
ran up a white flag and agreed to end
hostilities for the day. I pulled out my troops
from the flower beds, brought back the dead
to life, then boxed them all and went indoors.

There wasn't much for tea and when
I complained Mum snapped, 'I thought you said
there's a war on, and how am I supposed
to bring supplies through a battle zone?'

Later I watched the news on TV.
It seemed there was a war on everywhere.
Perhaps I'll declare an outbreak of peace tomorrow!

Monster Crazy

Everyone here has gone Monster Crazy,
even those who are normally lazy,
binoculars raised, though the view may be hazy,
everyone here has gone Monster Crazy.

So come on Nessie, give us a wave,
don't stay hidden in your underwater cave.
You're the talk of the town, the darling of the press,
it wouldn't be summer without you in Loch Ness.

Just come on up and prove that you're there,
some time or other you must surface for air,
somebody's camera will photograph you,
proving, at last, if you're one hump or two!

Everyone here has gone Monster Crazy,
even those who are normally lazy,
binoculars raised, though the view may be hazy,
everyone here has gone Monster Crazy.

Just waggle your flipper or flip your tail,
make some fisherman's face turn pale
as you lift your head to look at the view,
there are hundreds waiting to interview you.

Just one word Nessie, go on be a pet,
can't you stop playing hard to get?
You could be on TV, you'd have lots of money,
with American tourists calling you 'Honey'!

Everyone here has gone Monster Crazy,
even those who are normally lazy,
binoculars raised, though the view may be hazy,
everyone here has gone MONSTER CRAZY!

Baby Paul

When our teacher returned to work,
she came with her new baby.

'A baby shouldn't be any bother,' she said.
'I've looked after you lot for months!'

And baby Paul was pretty good –
slept through assembly, dozed during story.

We all kept finding excuses
to take a peep, jiggle the pram.
'Can I wind him Miss?'

It must have been confusing for baby Paul
with one mother and thirty-two minders.
Then once he started smiling,
we were hooked . . .

We played to an audience of one,
made silly noises,
smiled and laughed, giggled and gurgled,
cooed and tickled.

Even the tough ones
were twisting their faces to strange grimaces,
just to see who could
make Paul smile the longest!

Anyone who forgot their PE gear
had to push baby Paul
round the playground.

Lots of the girls were forgetting theirs
on purpose . . .
So we made up a rota.

The other kids said we were soppy,
all we'd talk about was Paul.
'You've gone potty,' they'd say.
But we were happy, changing nappies.

Other kids had hamsters, goldfish or tadpoles
to look after,
but baby Paul was a big hit
in our class!

Clubs

Who wants to join our club (club)?
Who wants to join our club?

There's a club for those who break all the rules club,
a club for those who play around in school club.
A join us if your teacher thinks you're good club,
a couldn't, but I really wish I could club.

Who wants to join our club (club)?
Who wants to join our club?

There's a parents always drive you round the bend club.
a don't trust your sister with your boyfriend club,
A club for those who hate soppy love stuff club
and a club for those who like being rough club.

Who wants to join our club (club)?
Who wants to join our club?

There's a hate going out in the rain club,
a don't you think your brother is a pain club.
A no one else, strictly me and you club,
a fan club for dishy Andrew club.

Who wants to join our club (club)?
Who wants to join our club?

There's a no boys, only girls allowed club,
a say it loud, we're naughty and we're proud club.
A stop the boys stamping on slugs club,
a club for those who like joining clubs club.

Who wants to join our club (club)?
Who wants to join our club?

How Can I?

How can I wind up my brother
when I haven't got the key?

How can I turn on my charm
when I can't even find the switch?

How can I snap at my mother
when I'm not a crocodile?

How can I stir up my sister
when I'm not even holding a spoon?

How can I pick up my feet
and not fall to the ground on my knees?

How can I stretch my legs
when they're long enough already?

Parents! – They ask the impossible!

Shoot the Messenger!

On playground duty, while sipping her tea,
Miss Martin told us stories.

'Long ago,' she said, 'if he brought bad news,
they used to shoot the messenger.

This bringer of bad tidings,
message hidden, horse hard-ridden,
would burst upon the scene
with news of some huge defeat
in battle.

And the first response would be,
pretend it hadn't happened,
make out they hadn't heard,
shoot the messenger,
forget his words.'

We listened, open-mouthed.
Miss Martin was smart,
her story must be true.

'Now,' she said, 'I've a job for someone.

Who wants to go to the staff room
to tell the teachers
it's end of break?'

Parent-free Zone

Parents please note
that from now on,
our room is
a 'Parent-free Zone'.

There will be no spying
under the pretence
of tidying up.

There will be no banning
of television programmes
because our room
is a tip,

no complaints about noise,
or remarks about the ceiling
caving in.

No disturbing the dirty clothes
that have festered in piles
for weeks.

No removal of coffee cups
where green mould
has taken hold.
(These have been left there
for scientific research purposes.)

No reading of letters
to gain unauthorized information
which may be used against us
at a later date.

No searching through school bags
to discover if we've done our homework
or unearth forgotten notes.

Our room is a 'Parent-free Zone'
and a notice is pinned to the door.

But just a minute,
there's something wrong . . .

MUM – WHY HAVEN'T YOU MADE OUR BEDS?

Abducted by Aliens

When Jack came back to school
after one day's absence, unexplained,
he went and told his teacher
he'd been abducted by aliens.
She told him not to be so daft,
but he gave us all the details –
what the spacecraft had looked like,
how extra-terrestrials kidnapped him
then carried him on to their ship.
And Jack told his story
again and again. 'When they landed,' he said,
'I was terrified, couldn't move,
I nearly died, then a blade of light
cut the night in two, trapped me
in its beam so I couldn't see. I felt
arms that were rubbery wrapped around me,
like the coils of our garden hose.

And I don't recall anything more
till I found myself back on the ground
while rasping voices were telling me
that everything I saw they would see,
that everything I heard they would hear,
that everything I ate they would taste.
And I know they're out there watching me,
in some intergalactic laboratory,
I'm a subject for investigation
constantly sending back information,
a bleep that bleeps on a bank of screens,
abducted by aliens, tagged and then freed.'

'What nonsense you talk,' his teacher said.
'Take out your books, who's ready for maths?'
But Jack couldn't make his figures come right.
If communication works both ways, he thought,
then he might benefit too –
Maybe aliens could help solve his multiplication!

The Bombsite

When I was young
I was always told
you can play outside,
you can play in the road,
you can play in the garden,
you can play on the grass
but don't go down to
the bombsite,
the bombsite,
the bom-tiddly-om-pom bombsite.

But one day our ball
crossed over the line
and someone had to
fetch it this time,
and the straw I drew
from my mate's fist
was my ticket
to the bombsite.

Warning bells
were sounding alarms,
I needed a couple
of lucky charms.
I knew the road
to kingdom come
was a direct route
to the bombsite,
the bombsite,
the bom-tiddly-om-pom bombsite.

Over I climbed,
holding my breath,
my heart thump-thumping,
scared to death
should anything hidden
be shaken awake
as I tip-toed about
in the bombsite.

I reached for the ball
and threw it out,
then eased myself back
as I heard someone shout:
'Get away from there,
you'll get yourself killed,'
and I clambered clear
of the bombsite,
the bombsite,
the bom-tiddly-om-pom bombsite.

My mates had vanished
really fast,
when our local copper
came cycling past.
He said he'd be round
to tell my dad,
how he caught me down
at the bombsite.

He called on us
that very same night,
his visit timed
to give me a fright,
but although I stood
expecting the worst,
he never mentioned
the bombsite,
the bombsite,
the bom-tiddly-om-pom bombsite.

But the very next week
the bombsite blew,
two cats on a
midnight rendezvous
lost every one
of their eighteen lives
in a scuffle out
on the bombsite.

I carried the secret
and tried to hide
the knot that
tied me up inside,
how I might have lost
my only life
on that crack-brained date
with the bombsite,
the bombsite,
the bom-tiddly-om-pom bombsite.

Next Door's Cat

Next door's cat lost
a couple of lives tonight.
Serve him right for
hanging around our pond,
seeking some fresh fish dish
to supplement his diet.

So out I crept behind the shed,
then slid on my belly, crocodile style,
while my target eyeballed the pond.

And I let him have just one more moment
of peace and contemplation,
before I let him have it . . .

I LEAPT and I ROARED,
I HOLLERED and I YELLED,
I WARDANCED and I SCREAMED,
I YAHOOED and I SCREEEEEEEEEEEEECHED . . .

And I *swear* I saw a miracle
out there in our back garden,
when next door's cat *walked on water*
to escape the wrath of a demon.

Puzzle

I thought I was the biggest child
in our little family,
but Mum says Dad's the biggest child
so where does that leave me?

There Are More Ways of Beating a Bully Than Biffing Him One.

Trevor was a bully, everyone knew,
he had flying fists and if one of them flew
in your direction, you'd know it all right,
he'd feint with his left and jab with his right.

He called kids names which upset them as well
and his favourite taunt was to say, '*YOU SMELL* –

of horse manure and mouldy cheese
of unwashed socks and leftover peas,
You smell, in fact you really stink,
you smell like a yeti, you're the missing link!'

Then Gavin decided, with his friend Malc,
to teach Trev a lesson and a can of talc
was opened and poured over Trevor's head,
and we listened, amazed, as Gavin said,

'*YOU SMELL*, in fact you really reek,
you won't need a bath until next week,
you stink of perfume sprays and soap,
of flowers and scented envelopes.'

'Well Trevor,' Malc said, 'you smell really sweet,
what a gorgeous pong as you stroll down the street.'
Then Trevor let out an enormous yell
and everyone scattered, racing pell-mell.

'We have other ways,' I heard Malc call,
'to beat a bully and we'll try them all
testing them out one by one on you,
not talc next time, but cold brown stew!'

Fishy!

At the Sea Life Centre
there were plenty of fish,
floating and gliding or
chasing about,
but although we saw
fish tails and fish scales,
teeth and mouths,
whiskers and fins,
we didn't see any
fishfingers!

Remote Control

When first we had a remote control for our TV,
Dad always used to sit on it so the screen went blank
or keep changing channels as he shifted his weight.
Our dog used to carry it off to his basket
then growl when anyone stooped to ask for it back.
Mum tidied it away, somewhere different each day,
while little brother made it a *never-to-be-without* part
of the mammoth Lego space station that consumed his room.
Grans and grandads failed to spot it,
knocked it off or sent it spinning.
Our neighbour's baby tried to wash it
and burglars, too, once tried to flog it!

But now we're into overload, we sit and shuffle
remote controls, the stereo and the video,
satellite channels too, and something Dad brought home
called DAT, which he used for a bit and then said, 'That's that,
can't make head or tail of this!'

But when Mum sits down to watch TV, aims the controls
and hears a succession of *blimps* and *beeps* and *blips*,
she closes her eyes and sinks back in despair.
All these gadgets just serve to confuse
when you can't even change to channel three for the news.

Lost Property Box

In our lost property box
there are socks with holes in
and shoes minus laces,
stand-up figures
without any bases,
a faded T-shirt
from Lanzarotte,
a greatest hits tape
by Pavarotti,
once-champion conkers
shrunken with age,
a mystery book
without the last page,
sandwich boxes
with last month's bread in,
PE shorts,
I wouldn't be seen dead in,
unloved toys and
mislaid gloves,
a Christmas card with
two turtle doves,
red underpants,
decidedly manky,
a barely used
lace-edged hanky,
a love letter
from David Pratt
to his girlfriend Sally,
what about that!

And right at the bottom,
what I'm looking for,
the sports shirt I borrowed
from the boy next door . . .

Perhaps he won't bash me
now I've found it!

Mind that Dog!

Just watch it or Rufus will get you,
he'll sort you out in a flash,
he'll make you move so fast
you'll win a medal in the half-mile dash.

Just watch it or Rufus will get you,
he's nabbed many children before,
he'll knock you down and shove you around
then leave you flat on the floor.

Rufus likes to show who's boss
but worse, far worse than this,
is when Rufus pins you down on the ground
and gives you a slobbery kiss!

Tests

If there were tests in complaining
then my brother would get full marks.
If there were tests in moaning and groaning
he'd be way out in front, no doubt.
If there were tests in arguing or fighting,
in getting his own way,
he'd win hands down any day.
If there were tests in being a pain,
in shouting or pouting,
in throwing a wobbly,
in tricking his mum or kicking his sister,
in fussing and feuding and falling out,
I know he'd be top of his class.
But give him a test in maths
and you'll only make yourself ill!
My brother's an ace at complaining
but his knowledge of figures is nil!